Geoff Gibson
I wanted to be
a Part of Things

By

Geoff Gibson
Richard Burkitt

I WANTED TO BE A PART OF THINGS
Geoff Gibson's Story

This is an honest and moving account of a child who fell victim to alcoholism and his struggle, through adolescence and into adulthood, to overcome it. Geoff's story, though tragic, is in parts humorous and ultimately, as he achieves sobriety, carries a message of hope in his continuing commitment to help others.

Beneath the surface lies a stark reminder of the failings within our society, where young children can 'slip through the net' and where bureaucracy and an emphasis on qualifications supersede the worth of 'caring' people and common sense.

For those who suffer with an addiction, for family and friends of addicts and for people who want to help, including those working within 'the system' who have become 'bogged down' with bureaucracy, this is an excellent read.

Louie Elizabeth Parker
June 2012

This book is dedicated to John and Janet
& Rab and Marion who all bothered with me,
when everyone else had given up.

Glossary

The Immortals: The older boys who know everything you need to know and alcohol and drugs and girls

The Gestapo: The clever kids who use long words and seem to speak a different language

The Titans: Those who control our vocabulary and tell us what we are allowed to say. They work in the social services or hidden in some dark room deep in the council building.

TEXT
Copyright
Geoff Gibson
Richard Burkitt
June 2012

ISBN
978-1-905787-31-9

To JOHN + MARGO
THANKS FOR ALL
THE HELP
Geoff

My Family

I was born on 22nd July 1965. I came from quite a loving family in Kessock Avenue in Inverness in the Highlands of Scotland. I was the second of three brothers. This was the poorest area of Inverness known locally as the Ferry because the boat to and from the Black Isle used to cross there. It was a tough sort of place but it had its own close community. My parents worked hard but didn't have much money. In those childhood days there wasn't much drink in the house. My father would go for an occasional pint at New Year time maybe and a few other times.

My father's parents, Granny Grace and Grandad Magnus, lived next door to us. Magnus was a French polisher at first and then a taxi driver. He knew a lot about fishing and hunting . He knew the times of the tides and it was Magnus Gibson who taught the locals how to fish. He used to tell a story that impressed me as a young boy. He said as a young man he went to fish in the Black Isle where he used to sit near an old fisherman who seemed to be a kindly old man. One day my Grandfather asked him what his work was and the kindly old man said he was the local hangman. My grandfather said he never went fishing there again.

My grandmother, Grace Campbell, had been a music teacher down in London and up here she taught Ceilidh music and was well respected. She taught a few of the top Scottish stars how to get the notes right. My grandparents died when I was quite young. I wished I could have seen more of them.

My father was James Leslie Gibson. He was a long distance lorry driver and drove a 38 ton Scania lorry. He seemed always to be exhausted but sometimes on the local run he took me on the trailer.

People said he had the healing gift. He cured people no one else could cure with his gifted hands and his ability to keep the blood flowing.

My mother was Madeline Mackay. She was a hard worker. My father met her in a café. She was ill often when I was young and, this, along with my grandparents getting ill, made me feel insecure but none of this is any excuse for what happened to me.

AT SCHOOL

I'm not sure why but when I was young I never felt I fitted in, even at home. I remember being nervous with people and awkward and never knowing what to say. When people came round I sneaked into the background.

I hated school. I always felt left out but the really big problem was that I couldn't read. I couldn't fathom out a thing about reading. The shape of letters meant nothing to me but then what would I expect? I just knew I didn't fit in.

People didn't know much about dyslexia in those days. All my school life I sat at the back and prayed that no one would ever ask me to do anything, and, most of the time, they didn't.

I fell miles behind the other pupils and there was no help at Primary school. On reflection, there must have been but let's just say it never got through to me. The constant fear of having to read or write made me completely withdrawn. I went through the whole of Merkinch Primary and Inverness High School without ever finding a teacher who got through to me. That was it. I couldn't read or write a word and that must be because I was stupid. I gave up hope of conquering reading and hid at the back of the class.

THE HOLIDAYS

Please don't suppose there were no happy times. There was always the holidays. For two wonderful weeks a year we went to stay with my mother's parents in Bettyhill in Sutherland. There was an incredible peace there and no one asked me to read. You just heard the sea and the stillness of the night. By the time you got used to it, it was time to go home. We'd feed the chickens and my Granny once gave me salt to put on the rabbit's tail. On reflection I think she just wanted me out of the house. I came back crying because I couldn't catch the rabbit. They all laughed at me. We used to walk three miles over the sands to get to the nearest shop. Walking in the countryside is such a beautiful thing to do. I should have done more of that.

Although they only lasted for those two short weeks, holiday times are my very best memories. A particular memory comes to me of an uncle who lived with Granny up in Bettyhill. I was in awe of him. He seemed like someone from Mars. My parents told me that my uncle was one of the first to get into the paratroopers. There is a story in the Bible about the shepherd who would risk his own life to rescue the missing sheep. On a good day my Uncle Neil seemed to us like that. He talked as if he was invincible. For us children he was the toughest, strongest superman we had ever met.

Uncle Neil had moods. Sometimes he talked sense to us about football and life and his dreams. Other times he became aggressive and frightened us and we were warned to keep out of his way. One day I was caught smoking his pipe so he gave me a large glass of brandy and was amazed to find I wasn't sick. I didn't like the taste but it gave me a giddy feeling that, for some reason, I liked. I didn't like it enough to want any more just yet but I was not sick. So he gave me a cigar and then at last I was very sick.

One day Neil took me out in a car when he must have been worse for drink. He asked me to change the gears. That was frightening to me. It was a team effort to get home.

Neil often looked at me strangely because perhaps he saw in me a kindred spirit. I was one day to become what he already was – an alcoholic.

Meeting the Immortals

I had an older brother and a younger but I spent most of my time with a friend called Sean.

When I was eight I went up with some of Sean's friends. These were older boys and, for Sean and I, these were the Immortals, boys we looked up to and came to worship. We went to a place called the Rockies. That was my first experience of addiction. They gave me a crisp bag with glue in it and I started sniffing it. It was a strange feeling but for me it was a good one. I felt I was fitting in with the boys. We all laughed together. We just rolled about and laughed and never before that moment had I ever really remembered laughing like that before. I felt I was a part of things and my years of tense awkwardness caused this horrible glue to be my friend.

I learned from the Immortals some essential information that day, like what girls were for and where babies came from. Looking back the information was a little flawed. I learned later that kissing alone does not produce babies but who cared if it made sense? These were the Immortals and they knew everything. They knew about stuff, about glue and cigarettes and even alcohol.

There were, however, no Immortals around when I first got drunk on alcohol.

Alcohol

My first experience of proper drinking was when I was nine. I was in Sean's house. His parents had a drinks cabinet and we decided to have a drop of each one. We got very drunk. We accidentally broke the cabinet and for some reason that only the strange logic of a drunk child would know, we decided to throw the drinks cabinet out of the window. Then we were both sick on the living room floor. When Sean's parents came back there was mayhem. They were round seeing my parents the next day and I was told never to meet with Sean again.

The resolve of my parents to keep us apart did not last very long. Anyway it was impossible to keep watch on us all the time. Soon we were back being friends again and I got Sean drunk a few more times.

I still didn't like the taste of spirits at all nor wine nor beer but I liked what it did to me. It made me feel a part of things. After drinking alcohol I felt normal, that this was my true self. It made me feel special and different and outgoing instead of the introvert that I had been before.

We got our drink from various places but we were mainly supplied by one particular older boy with what they now call 'learning difficulties, who didn't really know what he was doing but he bought drink for us often.

In school I never bothered anyone but Sean was the hardest man in High School and he kept me safe. At that stage Sean could take it or leave it more than me. I was already an addict before I left Primary School but Sean became one much later as an adult. He's doing fine now though. He's a landscape gardener and one of the best there is.

I used always to drink so much that I felt ill but I still wanted to drink the next day. This is what makes things different for the budding alcoholic. Most people drink less after their first experience of the nausea drinking can give you but I needed to drink alcohol to be who I was. I had an identity now. I was one of the lads, one of the hardest of all the lads, not because I drank. I often concealed that. I was the hardest because that is how drinking made me feel.

Death in the Family

I was still young when my Granny Grace died. I was hugely upset because I 'd not thought much about death. I was told her heart had just given up. Granny had always been there and now she wasn't and I found this difficult to bear. It certainly didn't stop me drinking.

Tragically my grandfather now took to drink himself. If he could have killed himself he probably would have done but instead he managed to drink himself to death within only two months.

I wouldn't dare to go near the house after Granny died and my grandfather was drinking. I was, in my young mind, trying to imagine what was going on in the house. All we heard was cursing and tears from next door. It was one of the unhappiest times of my childhood.

When my grandfather died I felt even worse because I hadn't seen him. I hadn't known what to say. I cried through the funeral and continued to drink with my friends.

I only learned to cope with death quite recently. One of the things that helped was when I managed to get gravestones for my grandparents and now, once again, I sit and talk to them.

Police Trouble

My first encounter with the police was when I was eleven and they caught me drunk one night. I ran away but the next day they came to the door to visit my house. My parents were very angry. The need to drink caused me to meet more and more often with the Immortals. They were even older now and I was learning more stuff. The Immortals would steal cars and take them over to the recreation ground where we would all learn to drive. I was given a shot at driving. So I first learned to drive when I was twelve years old in the recreation ground down the Ferry.

The problem with drinking is you feel wretched in the morning. That terrible advice to take the hair of the dog, to drink some more alcohol to recover, has been the cause of many an alcoholic. By the third year in High School, it is what I did every day. I woke up and I drank spirits or heavy duty lager or four crown wine for breakfast.

I had to be careful though. I needed to drink enough to be able to cope with school but not so much as to make the teachers send me home.

Drink gave me the confidence to talk to people. I wanted to be that person who could talk to the guys and talk to the girls, and, when I had a drink in me, that is who I was.

I met a new friend in High School. He was a rich kid. Every day he was pulling out of his pocket £10 notes and I'd go up town with him and I started to miss more and more school.

SECONDARY SCHOOL AND THE GREEN HUT

In the Highlands of Scotland those were not the days of special needs or even of remedial classes. What the school needed was a place for someone to babysit their most difficult pupils whilst the rest attempted some education.

The pupils that didn't fit in or were disruptive were sent to the green hut.

The green hut was a little bit away from the school and I suppose we were out of sight and out of mind. Miss Boyd was our green hut teacher. She was a lovely old lady, I suppose, but her job seemed to be to give the other teachers peace rather than teach us anything herself. We were sent to the green hut three times a week but none of us really knew why at the time. I just knew I had never fitted in and this was just proof of that. Strangely, however, the green hut was in a way a solution to that problem too. For the green hut is where they sent the bigger boys that I looked up to - the Immortals, the ones who knew the stuff I wanted to know.

The green hut had an advantage for us, being out of the way. It was behind the green hut where we all learned to smoke. That's also where I learned the facts of life, properly this time. I learned how you make babies.

I thought the older kids were so clever. They knew about sex and cigarettes and girls and stealing bikes and cars. They were indeed immortal beings who knew far better than any of the teachers the things I needed to know.

The Drink Sets In

By the time I left Merkinch Primary I was drinking every day but it was not until I was a year or two into High School that I started having withdrawal symptoms.

From the third year onwards I was drinking in secret. I was able to get drink because of my rich friend and all his money but even my friend didn't know that I was drinking also on my own. I would get out of bed and put some drink into my bag and try to get outside the house as fast as possible. I would drink on my way to school and later we'd go down to the place called the Islands, by the River Ness in Inverness, at all times of day to drink.

No one ever thought of me as being ill or as having an illness. I was just bad and abusing alcohol. I even convinced myself that I was just bad. It never occurred to me that I was not in control of what I was doing.

One day I was feeling a bit rough and next to the school there arrived a huge drinks lorry. They were taking drink off one side of the lorry whilst we took drink off the other side. We had a massive drinking session at the Islands that day.

There was sometimes up to fifteen of us. There we learned from the older guys more about life and we all laughed a lot. There was so much letting go of tension even if, in the end, most of us were very sick. It all seemed so much better than school. The Immortals told wonderful stories and we all laughed and laughed. The Immortals had all made love countless times and knew everything. At first the stories about girls were wild and imaginative but later real girlfriends started to join us. We had practical lessons in talking to girls and a whole lot more.

The Gestapo get Prizes on Prize-giving Day

There was always that group of kids at school who knew about maths and the other subjects and talked with long words. We didn't like them. The Immortals, for some reason, called them "the Gestapo". I know that's the wrong name altogether but we just knew from old war films that this was a group we didn't like. Just like the Gestapo in those old films they often used funny English and strange words and were set apart from us.

Looking back, I suppose they must have been frightened of us but I envied them because they could read and write and speak about stuff that we didn't understand, and they didn't need a drink just to be able to be themselves.

They were cut off and totally different from us. We didn't understand their lives and they didn't understand ours. On prize-giving day they got the prizes and we got the green hut. I do remember one good year though.

I remember once when Inverness High School prize-giving day was going on at school, the rich boy, the Immortals and me all went to this posh restaurant in town. I was fourteen by then but with the bigger boys we all passed for 16, so we ordered champagne and toasted the school and our teachers and thought of all the Gestapo receiving prizes whilst we ate steak and mushrooms and pudding and stuff. We gave each other pretend prizes as the real prizes were handed to the Gestapo at school. That was a wonderful occasion!

Don't suppose though that drinking was always a joyful thing. Most of my friends could take it or leave it. They drank less as they made themselves sick but I needed more and more to satisfy my addiction. In the end I needed the alcohol more than I needed my friends. They abused alcohol but I had become an alcoholic. This is a different matter altogether. You had to drink more and more each day to satisfy your addiction whilst all the time your body was suffering.

Learning where to go to find drink, how to fool your parents and how to get a school note written became my fulltime occupation. Luckily the Immortals were brilliant at forgery.

At Work

I had been thinking of going into the army but I don't think I would have lasted one day so my first job came about in an unexpected way.

As soon as I left school we moved to live in Kinmylies, a different part of Inverness where hundreds of houses had been built, sprawling all over the place with little regard for community. There was some sort of attempt at landscape gardening going on over the fence and to my amazement one of the workers was my old school friend Sean.

I pestered the foreman every day until he gave me a job and there was my cash supply to get drink. I got paid on Thursdays. So on a Thursday night we would go out drinking, On my own I would drink a half bottle of whisky and then we would go to a bar and keep on drinking until we got put out. Then there were parties and more drink. Then on Friday you had to drag your body into work.

It so happened the charge-hand was an alcoholic so he felt rough in the morning and got Sean and I to do the driving of the van. We had no licence and we were full of alcohol too but we drove to Aviemore and other places. For lunch the charge-hand would drink and that enabled him to stop shaking and able to drive home.

One day Sean and I decided to turn the van round which had a trailer on it. So we went up a country track to look for a turning place. For fun we decided to go at speed. There was a man with a push bike who had to jump into the bushes. He was waving his fists in the air which at the time we thought was quite funny.

I was egging Sean on to go faster. We ended up going three hundred feet down a bank and the tow bar of the trailer went through the front window of the van. We crawled out, found ourselves on the A9 and hitched a lift on a scaffy wagon back to Inverness. We were lucky to be alive.

Meanwhile the charge-hand and the police started searching for bodies. When, later, they found us alive, they were furious we had left the scene of an accident. My father and mother went off their head. I felt smug because I knew the police couldn't charge us because it was a private track.

The policeman laughed and said, "There's just one detail you have forgotten. What about the man on the push bike? "

Sean and the charge hand and myself all got sacked. In the morning I had Carlsberg Special for breakfast again.

Making Money

Sean and I started working for a different landscaping firm. We were doing this huge patio and landscaping the land. It was a really big job and we were there for a couple of weeks. We were drinking all the time and getting rougher and rougher. We had an idea that we would go up and finish the job off. There were around 15 slabs to finish. We got most of this done and we told the householder that our boss was away and we should receive the payment. The next morning we came back and finished the job and received £2000 in cash. We were unbelievably drunk driving home, We damaged the van which we fixed with a hammer!

Some of you may not believe that it is possible to spend £2000 in less than a week on drink. This is how you do it. You start with a bottle of the best whisky three times a day for breakfast, lunch and dinner, washed down with the very best food in the very best restaurants whilst your boss is losing his mind frantically searching for you. The important thing at nights is to not to answer the door and keep the phone switched off.

He eventually caught up with us at Sean's House. He had been stalking the house and waited for a opportune moment when we opened the door. Now, as we have told you before, Sean was a tough bloke. So Sean and I stood there like two guilty schoolchildren waiting to be punished, but the Boss was not physically strong enough to give us a good hiding though we knew we deserved it. To his credit, our Boss coped with us and didn't even sack us. I suppose, looking back, we were quite good workers even when drunk. But the drink was becoming less of a joke. Because of the drinking my body was shutting down and sustaining a job became more and more difficult.

Becoming More Acquainted with Death

I had a good friend from school, a gentle person who made me laugh with his jokes and stories. I hung about with him after we left school. He got hit by a car one day and died in the local hospital. That rocked me to the ground because this was the wrong order of things. Grandparents die first not people of your own age. This death really affected me and I can understand how others feel when people die before their time.

My mother had been ill with lung cancer for a few years but it was around about this time that she died too.

In the later stages of her illness my father started drinking. He never had anyone in the house. There weren't so many nurses or carers about in those days. The caring for my mother took a great toll on him and because of my drinking I could not comfort him.

I was drinking in the Muirtown Hotel when I heard that my mother had died. I had been no help to my father but when she died I flew into a rage and started blaming the hospital for everything.

I was on the phone full of anger and bitterness. Looking back I feel a bit sorry for hospitals when people blame them for stuff. I was maybe blaming them for death itself when I should have been blaming God but I was also blaming them because of my own guilt. To this day, it hurts me that I never made amends with my mother for all the heartbreak I had caused. I vowed that day that I would give up drinking and one day soon be able to help my father.

More Dicing with Death

I did not give up. My alcoholism grew worse. I diced with death more and more often. I was up town with my friend and I managed to push him right through a plate glass window. We were lucky. We got away with a £400 fine.

I had a job as a scaffolder. I hated heights and if I'd been sober I would never have gone up, but there I was on high roofs walking on thin wobbly narrow planks carrying heavy slates. Each step I took I was dicing with death but the drink made me feel invincible. The forty foot drop didn't trouble me at all.

One time I went up there without enough drink inside me and I have never been more scared. I prayed to the God you are only acquainted with during a near-death experience. When you have not had enough to drink you realise your mortality. Everything is fine until you look down and then the nausea sets in. I made it finally to the ground. From then on, if I hadn't drunk enough before I would not go up there for anyone. I would hide somewhere or go ill.

The job ran out there. I got a couple more jobs but gradually I became unable to work at all.

I was always sick in the morning, but if I got the first drink down, I could get to the shop and keep going for the day. If I could not get that first drink down I was sick as anything. I kidded on a few times that I was just normally sick. Sometimes I almost convinced myself.

Having Children

A few years earlier I had met my partner Janet at a party. I probably couldn't ever have met her sober. At that time I was convinced I needed the drink to have the confidence to talk to anyone and especially to women.

I met her most weekends from then on. She only knew me when I had the drink inside. For a long time I managed to hide the fact I had a problem. I was just on a good night out. I drank enough always to keep me level. I never knew Janet sober. I might have been a different person. The Geoff Janet knew had drink in him. For quite a few years I was just about able to keep my problem under control. We would go for a drink together and I would have two pints. What Janet didn't know was that during the day I had drunk half a bottle of whisky before breakfast and three or four Carlsberg specials in the morning. At Lunchtime I would have more whisky and three or four more specials in the afternoon.

We moved in together and had two children. All that time I concealed the amount of my drinking. I had invented many ways of hiding the drink. I would find a thermos flask and go off to work or go fishing. There would be tea on the inside of the flask but the rest of the flask was taken out so it could be filled with whisky. I developed other ingenious ways to hide my drinking. The best place of all was the garden shed. In my adulthood as in my school days a shed became a place of sanctuary. A shed was a man's place, nothing to do with women. I would hide the drink in boxes, under floorboards and lampshades, in burnt out washing machines and in the flower garden at the back. Occasionally Janet found some of it and little by little she came to understand that alcohol wasn't a hobby for me but a whole way of life.

I felt guilty deep down keeping all this secret from my partner. We never talked it through, but strangely, my partner felt guilty too. As my problem became more obvious to her, my poor partner thought that maybe I was drinking because of her, that somehow it was all her fault. This often seems to be what happens. The partner both blames herself for her partner's illness but also starts to cover for him or her and make excuses for them. One of the only honest moments in our relationship was when I told Janet that the illness was not her fault in any way at all. It was my fault and at last I admitted to someone other than myself that I had a problem.

When Janet told me she was pregnant, for a few weeks I did try harder to quit but I couldn't. The birth of my first child should have been a wonderful experience but I was so drunk and so ill that it almost passed me by. I was there at the birth and it was an experience that I wouldn't have missed and I did want to support my partner. It was a brilliant moment, and, at that very second, I was going to stop drinking forever.

I went cold turkey.   I had that intense craving for alcohol. This got worse and worse. I just felt terrible. I tried to lie down for a few hours then wake up with every nerve on edge. I felt dizzy and full of unknown fears and this lasted for days whilst at the same time I was vomiting and I could hardly stand up. I managed it. Everything was going to be all right . I would be the best father. I'd get a proper job and kiss my wife goodbye each morning and return tired but happy into her adoring arms. This idyllic dream lasted one week. God loves a trier!

You see, after the physical withdrawal, you have to cope with the stuff running around in your head. Living with yourself sober can be very hard. Your mind fills up with all the things you had blotted out for years. There are waves of guilt that are so difficult to bear without help. At that time I had no AA to help me, no help at all and no counselling. That's what you need to do - talk to someone, tell them how you're feeling.   It's terrible when you have lost your protective blanket and you cannot numb the pain and everything is so raw and tense. The worst times are when the bad stuff attacks you at night.

Regrets and fears flood in and your stomach turns over. The pain gets so bad you take a drink and this is madness because you're taking the thing that is killing you. The definition of insanity is doing the same thing over and over again but expecting different results.

By the time Janet had had a second child my problem was so obvious, I was never left alone with the children. It is one thing to know you have a problem but quite another to deal with it.

I did go through many other periods where I tried to stop drinking, especially because I wanted to please Janet, to be a regular guy and get married in a church. I went twice to see the minister and go through the rehearsal in Church and I vowed to give up drinking, but it was too painful. So my partner and I were never married. None of this was Janet's fault, though at the time I was blaming everyone else. The way that alcoholics can fool themselves into blaming others for everything that is wrong with their lives is what makes alcoholism so ugly.

Many people try to withdraw from alcohol using street valium. It cost about £1 a tablet then. I found the problem with the street valium was that it took a day to work. My few remaining drinking friends and I all shared prescriptions for the real thing from doctors who could be persuaded to prescribe it. If I took four or five tablets it calmed the nervous system down and stopped me fitting. However most people took valium to get an extra high with the drink.

There are Titans out there who control our vocabulary and tell us what we are allowed to say. They work in the social services or hidden in some dark room deep in the council building. They tell us that it is correct to talk of substance abuse, so, of late, we have not been able to talk about drug or drink addiction but only about substance or alcohol abuse. There are of course people who abuse alcohol and that is sad but I wasn't abusing alcohol. Instead alcohol was abusing me. I had to have it to stop the shakes.

The people I now work with need no jargon, no correct way of speaking. Addiction is the problem. I once had, and my friends have right now, the terrible debilitating illness of alcoholism. This is an illness that rules every minute of every waking day.

One day someone suggested that if I took heroin I would get rid of the shakes. So they took me to a flat and injected me with heroin. Many people talk of the overwhelming experience of euphoria at the first taste of heroin but you chase that experience for the rest of your days as your life is wrecked bit by bit.

I took heroin twice but luckily for me it just made me sick, really sick, my whole body cried out against it. Heroin is more expensive than drink and I would have needed a life of crime to pay for it.

The problem was that as I became unfit for work and had to live on benefits, my partner Janet found it difficult to cope with me. My problem was impossible to hide. I was now home all the time and not even the garden shed could hide the fact that I had a problem.

I couldn't always get the money I needed for drink and when I couldn't pay for the drink to remain in my system, not only did I get terrible withdrawal pains but, soon after my second child was born, I had my first seizure.

We were in the supermarket. I told my wife I didn't feel well but she wanted me to go shopping with her. Half way round I felt sick. Then I cant remember what happened next but I woke up in hospital. From that time on I had fits regularly, as often as once a week.

Janet didn't want to watch me killing myself. It's a hard life for the partner of an alcoholic. You sit there drunk and, as drunks do, repeat yourself over and over again and get stupidly emotional and sentimental about the smallest things. The trouble is you think you are normal when in fact most of what you say is total nonsense and the worst is you wont let it go but go on repeating all your worries till everyone leaves the room. Janet was good to me but there is a limit to what a partner can put up with.

I have seen so many relationships destroyed by alcohol. For many the very best thing to do is to separate otherwise that awful phrase - if you cant beat them join them - sets in and you became as sick as your partner. I was almost glad when Janet asked me to leave. I knew I wouldn't be putting her through any more pain. She was a good person and a decent mother and I needed to go. I moved in with my Dad.

I was shocked to find that my father's drinking had increased. He couldn't live without my mother. The last thing he needed was me back in his life. Little by little, his drinking increased and, worse, my two brothers joined in. So four alcoholics lived in that house by the canal beside Abdul's shop and whenever any of us had money, the drink was bought before any thought of food.

We had sessions when all four of us drank together along with a neighbour. There was a bit of singing and a lot of arguments. In our drunken haze we could only look back and remember with sadness the loving caring family we had once been.

In Search of Alcohol and Alcohol Friends

There was one time when a supposedly rich friend took me to a Chinese restaurant and we had a huge meal before my friend confessed that, actually, he had no money at all. He told me not to worry about it, but I was worrying. I didn't have enough drink inside me not to worry. So my friend ordered me two more pints and a whisky and then I didn't mind so much. My friend's plan was that you must find a time when all the waiters are busy. It may only be for a second or two but that is the time to choose.

The moment came and we rushed down the stairs and ran for it. Someone chased us down the stairs but we had made our escape and we got away with it, but I never talked to that friend again.

I didn't like cheating anyone, though sometimes it it seemed like harmless fun. Such a time was at the professional photographers' conference. This was at the Muirtown Hotel. I was desperate for a drink. I did my dressing up routine. It's strange how, if you put a tie on, everyone thinks you're ok even though there might be soup stains all over the shirt you are wearing.

So I put a tie on and borrowed a camera. I didn't know anything about cameras and I think it was the latest Kodak Brownie but it was ok with me. The tie did the trick!

I got into the room where free drinks were being dispensed. No one seemed to notice that my Brownie camera was not of the most professional type or they were too polite to say so. I learned that the way to talk to these professional folk is to ask questions and hope they don't ask you any back. So I chose a talkative fellow and asked him what his special secrets were and, as he droned on for what seemed like hours, I drank as much of the free drink as I possibly could. It seemed that many of the journalists were doing the same as me. No wonder they say that journalism and alcoholism go together.

On a very rare occasion somebody invited me out and we went up the town into a more salubrious place than I was used to. That night there were no roll ups. For the first time in years I smoked real cigarettes and even went for something to eat, which felt strange considering the way I was living. We didn't eat cheaply and I was afraid we would have to make a run for it when the bill came but luckily my friend said it was his treat. We went round a few of the better bars and ended up in a late opening club with snooker tables. My friend left and gave me money for a taxi. On the way out I saw this guy who asked me where the taxis were. I heard his Irish accent and I said, as a joke, you sound like Alex Higgins. He replied to my surprise, "Yes that's me." Then he asked me what my name was. He had a bottle of spirits in his hand and I asked if he was going to drink it all by himself. He said in his Irish accent, "Have a drop of that."

For thirty minutes we sat on the pavement and drank from that bottle. My friend Alex and I connected perfectly, talking the sort of stuff that only drunks appreciate. I told Alex he may have learned to play the game but I was a natural and could beat him any day. The truth is that world champion snooker player, Alex, was legendary for being a natural and gifted player, but he laughed out loud and he probably would have challenged me to a game if either of us could have stood up. Finally, as best I could, I walked my new best friend along to the taxi rank and helped him into the car. He gave me twenty pounds for a drink on him. In the back of the car he said to the taxi driver, "Take me to London." That was a journey of 700 or more miles but the taxi driver set off and that was the last I saw of my drinking chum Alex Higgins.

That was how it was for us alcoholics. There were days of loneliness and much abuse from the public but just occasionally you met a kindred spirit. I have seen drinking folk walking along the road, chuckling to themselves and having an imaginary conversation with a non-existent best mate. That conviviality is what so many alcoholics yearn for and so many non-alcoholics detest. Well, the great Hurricane Higgins was my best friend for half an hour and that was a major triumph in my desperate little world.

Another time at the Muirtown Arms I was sitting drinking, and, like all drunks, I needed someone to talk to. I went through to the lounge bar and in the corner they had a guitar and drums. There was a wee band singing. They took a break and I met a lady standing at the bar and asked if she'd like a drink. She and I started talking some usual nonsense. I wasn't chatting her up or anything. It was just a chat.

She told me she found me like a breath of fresh air and bought me several drinks as we laughed together. She told me she would get up and sing. I told her she couldn't do that or she'd be thrown out and I tried to drag her back. She told me she was going to sing a song and that was that. I begged her not to but she just laughed at me. She went over and sung and it was the sweetest sound I had ever heard.

She sang several songs. I was the only person in the bar apart from three strange looking blokes in green jackets near the door. The concert seemed to be for me. I was touched by this and stopped protesting that she was doing anything wrong, and, when she returned, I told her she was lucky not to be thrown out. I also told her she had a surprisingly nice voice and maybe, if she worked at it, she could make a living out of it rather than gatecrash gigs. She gave me a phone number and told me her name was Philomena Begley. She laughed and it was only then I realised that the folk in green jackets I had seen in the corner of the bar were her security guards and that she was a famous singer taking a break from her tour. Later I learned that she had sung that night in front of a packed-out audience at Inverness' celebrated Eden Court Theatre. Mind you I bet the concert wasn't as good as the private concert she gave me!

More Minor Triumphs

Even the most desperate life contains a few small victories. One day I managed to get hold of a very good quality bike and for a while I treasured that beautiful machine. It gave me much pleasure, but I was an alcoholic and sooner or later the day came when the only way to get money for drink was to sell the bike. The salesman knew I was desperate for a drink and bought the bike off me for a ridiculously low price. I went round for a few days brewing anger against the salesman. This played on my mind so much, I hatched a plan.

First I took enough whisky to make me feel normal, then I borrowed a suit and dressed up like Lord Lovat himself and sauntered back to the shop.

I had to wait till the shop was really busy. Then I walked round the back and saw my own bike newly polished for sale at five times the price they had paid me for it. So I seized the bike, took off the price label and then took it round to the front of the shop and sold it back to the same salesman. As I was looking so smart and normal he didn't recognise me. Thinking I was an upper class sort of chap he gave me a really good price. Justice was done.

Another day an infamous local family of Asbo fame were asking me for dope so I took the brown beads out of the large fake flower pot in a Town centre bar and charged them the full dope price. Somehow putting it in silver paper made it look real. Anyway he was too drunk to notice and paid the full price. I had to hide from that family for weeks but somehow I survived.

A triumphant day was the day of the watches. I was walking round town with a drinking friend. Who had bought a fancy new watch. I decided we should sell it to the pawnbrokers. Collect for Cash they are called and they usually cause misery to the poor with their hard hearted deals.

My friend allowed me to try to sell his watch. I said to the pawnbroker that the watch had been bought for three times the amount it actually was. To my amazement the man gave me £5 more than my friend had paid for it. I said I had more and that day I sold him 15 watches and made £75 profit. My friend and I had our drink money that day.

The Coal Trail

I was not getting on well with my father and so I resolved to go and make peace with him. I was very drunk. On the journey drunken logic was spinning in my head. I wanted a reconciliation with my father, so, on the way up to the house, there was a coal yard with a lorry outside. So you can guess what I got him for a gift.

There I was at midnight taking a huge bag of coal off the lorry and putting it on my back. This would be a loving gift for my father. If I hadn't been so drunk I could have got away with it but I had to put the bag on the ground. It was snowing and I dragged the bag round to the house. I managed somehow to empty it out into the coal bunker, with the bag left on top of it. I went to the door and was preparing my speech for my father but unfortunately, when I went in, my father was sleeping. I fell asleep too on the sofa and in the morning I heard my father raising his voice at the back door. There was no more snow that night but there was a clear trail from the coalman's lorry to my father's house.

Now the coalman was a big man and my father was no match for him. However, they soon worked out who the culprit was and the coalman was threatening to give me a good hiding. My father, God bless him, defended me and paid for his new delivered coal. Then, once the coalman had gone, he turned round and kicked me out of the house! It took him a while, actually six months, before he could laugh about it

The Strong Man

I used to meet the strong man up the town with my friend Kevin. He was the strong man because he had won prizes on the TV. He could push a Scania lorry ten yards but he also knew how to drink. What fascinated me with him was that he would have two fish suppers with extra chips resting on his lap as he drove home with one hand on the steering wheel and the other holding a large bottle of vodka. His hand covered the whole bottle.

The police would pull him over and try to arrest him. The tallest of the policemen would appear to be half his height. The story goes that the police flew in the air like matchstick men ending up scattered in various fields.

Little by little the wiser police persons realised that it was not a good idea to approach the strong man at night. They used to visit in the morning, tapping gently on the door and using their best police smiles and Sunday language. It was quite a sight to see the strong man sober, quite happy to let the nice humble police persons book him to rights and, like coachmen of old, offering a carriage to a gentleman, would escort him off to the cells.

At night I would tell the strong man that if he didn't buy me a drink I'd throw him out of the bar. People used to look round and fear for my life but the strong man roared with laughter and was our protector and if anyone else troubled us he would lift them up whilst sitting on their stool and growl at them.

A Police Chase and other Incidents

At first I wasn't completely homeless. I stayed on sofas, or, sometimes, if I begged enough my father would reluctantly let me spend a night at his house.

I had a motor bike when I was there. I had run out of insurance. The law had recently changed so you needed a licence for a 250cc bike. I took it to Muirtown Hotel, where I drank my usual amount. When I was coming out to go home on the bike, I started it up and the front light failed. The police were on the other side of the road and I made the sort of split decision you usually live to regret, to take off.

When they came after me in the car, I don't know if it was the sirens or the drink that caused the adrenalin to kick in. There was a high powered chase. My bike was tuned up and I went down paths and side roads while the police did their best to catch up with me. They nearly went into a fence which I just missed but I hit a footpath and the bike leapt in the air. I thought I would die but I managed to get the bike under control again and I somehow managed to get away. When they came round, I told them the bike was stolen and for some reason, (maybe my cherubic face!), they believed me.

Round about the same time there was another incident. I was driving a transit van with no licence, insurance or tax. The police were following me for some time. There was just the one policeman in the car. He indicated for me to pull over and came over to the van. I started talking to him. I got him all confused, talking such rubbish as came to my head and constantly changing the subject. After about twenty minutes he walked away scratching his head perhaps wondering if he had an alien experience. I drove away still with no insurance or licence or tax. On drink I was good at stories and that was one of my finest moments.

Abdul had Muirtown Stores. He had a new beer and he wanted to try it out. Who better than me! So I was one of the first people in Inverness to test out Tenants Super Lager. It was like Carlsberg Special but it went down a little bit easier. I didn't tell that to Abdul at first.

When the shop was busy I went back in and I said to him I wasn't sure. He told me to try another one. I waited outside and fifteen people came in. He looked really harassed and I did the same thing. I got four cans and enjoyed every one of them before he realised I was conning him. He was fuming because no one could con the great Abdul. He told me not to come back.

A Perfect Day? Working the System

I was needing more drink. I decided to go for a crisis loan.

You have to get up really early like 10 a.m, then make sure you get it right. You can ask for stuff like food and clothing but you don't go in smelling of drink for fear you will be found out.

That day, covered in after-shave and the sweet smell of strong mints, I put on one of my best performances. There has recently been talk of aggressive begging in our little part of Inverness but I wasn't that far down yet. That came later. I was still a good performer and in those days you didn't just talk on the phone, I could talk to a real person and this time I remember her name was Gill.

I told her about my need for food and clothing and how my shoes had holes in them. I did so well, I even felt sorry for myself. Gill said the loan was approved and I must come back at 2 p.m. I was delighted and I was sitting on a chair talking to my new friend Gill when I took a fit.

I landed on the floor and woke up in Raigmore Hospital very confused and feeling unwell. Then, little by little, I remembered the situation. The crisis loan! I had earned that money. My God I had earned that money! That was my Oscar winning performance. The nurse could not persuade me to stay in hospital. The lure of the crisis loan was so great. I could smell the whisky before I even got out of my bed. I made it back to the social just before closing time. They thought it was a miracle. How was it possible to be stretchered out of their place and then return so quickly. The desperate, overwhelming, urgent need for drink made it possible!

That day I received £37.00 in a postal order. I rushed round to Queensgate Post Office, got the cheque cashed, bought a quarter bottle of Whisky and headed for Gellions, a bar in the centre of Inverness. I went into the toilets because I was shaking too much to hold a pint. I just managed to get the top of the bottle of whisky off but I was shaking so much the bottle crashed against my teeth. The first mouthful made me sick but the second one stayed down. I breathed a huge sigh of relief. Now the shakes had stopped and I carried on drinking. I went to the market bar and someone put dope in my mouth. I ate it. I was so high I can't even remember being lifted. The joke that went round the Bar was that Geoff doesn't smoke dope, he eats it. Because it was a holiday weekend I stayed in those cells till the following Tuesday.

IN THE POLICE CELLS

I was so dry in the cells that my tongue was literally stuck to the roof of my mouth. I went through all the same pain I have spoken of before. I didn't shave for the judge because the shakes were too bad.

My performance before the judge was another Oscar winning event. I must have impressed him because he let me go with a warning. I had been informed that this was the judge who smiled but hated you smiling back so he smiled and I scowled and all went well.

One time I had nowhere to stay so I heard on the grapevine that you could get into the railway carriages to sleep. I did that for a few nights. On the way to the train station one night with a few of the violent boys we were approaching the railway club and one of the guys had a brilliant idea that we should all climb onto the roof and get back down again. Of course with my problem with heights I was a wee bit afraid and last to get on to the roof .

On the way back down the drainpipe I was struggling a bit when I heard some kind words, "I'll give you a hand down." There I was being carried in the arms of Sergeant Stewart from the local constabulary. He was not convinced that this was just a game of dares and decided to charge me with breaking in, until they checked the place over and found no damage and nothing missing. Nevertheless I spent another painful weekend in the cells, painful because of the shakes and the agony of craving for alcohol. The judge couldn't find my previous history and asked me if I'd been in trouble before. Well, as you can imagine, this was an opportunity for another performance. By the time I had finished with that judge I think he was ready to adopt me! I told him this was my first offence and that I was normally a decent sober upstanding chap with a wife and two small children to feed. He believed me and let me go.

Even my drinking friends were horrified and told me that lying to a judge was a serious offence. For weeks I was expecting to get lifted but it never happened.

Getting Lower

One time I begged Janet to let me have some time with the children. She trusted me to pick them up and take them to playschool. I made an honest effort not to drink that day. So I picked them up and dropped them off. On the way back I managed to reach the co-op and I felt that sickening feeling in my stomach. I knew a fit was coming so I sat down on the grass and passed out. I started coming round and I had a tremendous fright. I had lost my memory completely. My instinct told me not to move and stay where I was. So I just sat on the grass and it was terrifying. I had forgotten everything, even my own name.

Some kind stranger passed by and phoned the ambulance and my paramedic friends, who knew me by name now, took me to hospital. The children weren't picked up from playschool that day and that was the last time that I was ever entrusted with them.

The hospital reckoned that the fits were causing me some brain damage and wanted to keep me in for tests but, once again, I did my performance and there I was back at Abdul's shop with an Oscar in one hand and a Carlsberg Special in the other.

I began to believe that the only way to prevent a seizure was to keep drinking. My drinking had entered a different phase. Now I was drinking in order to prevent myself from having fits. So now you see, as I told you before, I wasn't abusing alcohol. Alcohol was abusing me. It had me completely in its power.

Alcohol had been my friend now it was my angel of death. My days were numbered and I was playing Russian roulette. Each time I took a drink it might be my last but if I didn't take a drink I might fit and die anyway. These were the unhappiest days of my life.

When I didn't have money I drank whatever I could right down to Brasso or perfume or cough mixture. One time I tried a can of cigarette lighter fuel but it made me very sick.

I moved back in with my father briefly but not even my Dad could put up with my drinking. He didn't need me to encourage him to drink. He had his own drink problem to deal with. We had an argument over one of my drunken rages and he asked me to leave. I couldn't get anyone to take me in. I was alone and homeless.

Mixing with the Violent Boys

When my father put me out of the house I had nowhere to go and my only friends were the other drunks I met on the street. These were the violent boys.

My life got worse. No one in their right mind would have mixed with the people I mixed with but all I wanted was to get a drink and I would sit with the meanest criminal if there was drink available. I wasn't scared of them but I marvelled at the insane hatred violent people have for so many minority groups, such as immigrants or homosexuals. No-one looks down more on others than people in the gutter. It was painful and ugly to be with them but I didn't care if there was half a chance of getting a drink.

Once or twice one of these violent folk thought I was weak and they could have power over me and, more than once, I was attacked, even propositioned for sex. The drink made me senseless but somehow afraid of no one. So I fought back. One guy took a knife to me and said he would cut my throat and I grabbed the knife out of his hand and I told him the next time he took out the knife he would be in the morgue. He got a fright because the drink had made me invincible.

The weakest are set upon in this sort of group. It's the only power that the drunk, with his life in a shambles, can have over others.

I remember one time when a lad took a group of us into his house. I left but the rest stayed. They took over that house for many months, putting the poor tenant out. He was so scared of them he became homeless himself. Most days I would have to protect my benefit or begging money and find more ingenious ways to hide it.

It wasn't my nature to be a bully or steal from others and I did not like the fighting. In the end it just seemed better to be alone.

Drinking seems to the young to be a social thing. It's about fun with everyone and laughter as it was in those early days with the Immortals on the Islands, but for the alcoholic, drinking finishes up a lonely thing. It destroys your family and all your relationships and leaves you degraded, humiliated and alone.

No Friends Left

I was sitting by the canal or lying down trying to sleep or walking about when it was too cold.   I was in my late twenties. I was so bad by this time that I cant remember some of the things that happened.   One person told me they had never seen anyone so young look so old and pathetic.

I know why people commit suicide. It's thinking that you wont have to cope with this pain any more. No more suffering. No more of the hell of living this life. It was a happy feeling, it made me smile.

One particular day I was fed up with the withdrawal and the begging, the endless search for money and the race against time to force down the drink before the seizure occurred. I'd just had another fit and I had no money left and I couldn't buy the drink to keep the seizures away. I   was thinking of smashing a window and grabbing some drink but I ended up walking along the road past my old friend Abdul's shop.   I thought of asking for tick but I didn't bother.   I had other plans. It was dark and it was raining. I heard a 38 tonner Scania lorry. I knew what it was because, as you know, my Dad used to drive lorries like that. When I first saw a Scania lorry I never imagined that my life would come to this. I tried to time it exactly right so that I would step into the road at exactly the right time but I even got that wrong. I longed for no more pain and no more fits and no more loneliness. The drink had become my lover but I wanted my lover dead.

One, two, three and I stepped right in front of the lorry and closed my eyes expecting to die but the lorry driver managed to put his brakes on and screech to a halt two feet in front of me.

I went up to the van driver who had wound down his window and I was raging. I was shouting at him and wanting to beat him up for not killing me. The lorry driver wound up the window, and, on his radio called for the police.

In the hospital later it took me four hours to convince the psychologist that I wasn't insane. It was another great performance. I was so good, I even surprised myself. I couldn't believe they would believe what I said but I had told so many lies I couldn't tell truth from reality. I even convinced myself that I was normal and this was going to be the first day of a new life. So I signed myself out of the hospital and put one deliberate step in front of the other intending to visit my father as the prodigal son and all would be well from here and forever.

Unfortunately my body had its own cravings and had other ideas and within twenty minutes I was buying Carlsberg Specials or was it Tenants Super Lager from Abdul's own little shop.

Not too long after that I landed in hospital again. I had gone back to my violent friends but I didn't have the strength any more to cope with their need for control. One of them hit me over the head with a piece of wood and this time, when I landed up in hospital, the hospital social worker did mention to me for the first time the name of Beechwood and someone was kind enough to take me there. This was the rehabilitation centre in Inverness where, in those more compassionate days, drunks could be taken to dry out.

When I arrived, there was a man called John who decided to take a risk with me. They told me later that I should have been dead and was too ill really to go in but John had taken pity on me.

Now that I work with drinkers all the time I realise how easy it is to walk on the other side of the street when I see a drunk. It often seems wiser to keep a distance especially if the drunk is emotional or violent or aggressively begging for money. But now, where possible, at least I give the speech. I tell the drunk that there is hope, that I have been helped and he or she can be helped too, that there is the AA and places like Beechwood and the For the Right Reasons Project that can help them if and when they are genuinely ready to be helped. It may not be any use to them at that moment but later it can stick in their mind and guide them to the right place.

Anyway I stayed in the drying-out centre at Beechwood for two weeks. One day someone gave me a tea shirt and this simple act brought me to tears because I had been alone for quite a while.

When I came in they had to cut my boots off my feet which, with the socks, were stuck fast. I was in a terrible state but by some miracle my liver survived.

The Prodigal Son

It took me a few goes in Beechwood before I finally gave up the drink for good. I was taken over to the sixteen week rehabilitation course. They taught me like a child how to wash and keep clean and keep the room tidy. You are not allowed out for the first few weeks but the first opportunity I got was, for once, not to go to the off licence but at last to go back to my father, ask his forgiveness and tell him how well I was doing.

I was so pleased to be coming home to my father sober. I felt a great happiness as I set out to his house and I knew, I just knew he would be so proud of me. I knew he was still drinking but I would talk to him and see him through the shakes. I was the prodigal son retuning and all manner of things would be better.

When I got to my father's house a great shock awaited me. There were police everywhere. My father and my brother were nowhere to be seen.

Gradually I learned that my father had died after a long drinking session with my brothers. One of the young police officers stopped me and told me I couldn't go into the house. He was cold and officious. I was about to knock him down and go into the house but an older policeman came over, put his arm on my shoulder and explained with some gentleness why I couldn't go in. I just cried in his arms.

It seems that my two brothers and Dad had been drinking all night and fell asleep but in the morning they couldn't wake Dad up. My brothers were taken to the police station and my eldest brother put in the psychiatric hospital at Craig Dunain.

I had to look after the funeral. At the funeral I nearly fell into the coffin with the shock of everything. It shouldn't have been like this. My father had not been a drinker as long as I. It seemed that the drink gradually set in but I'd no idea it was so bad and I was in great shock.

I went back to see my friend Abdul at the Muirtown stores. My whole body and soul was telling not to do it but I asked for a Tenants Super strength and I drank it there and then. It made me feel worse because now I was in no position to help my brothers who were both in need of so much help.

I didn't go back to Beechwood. I wandered about for three or four days in a land of hell all of my own making. I wished that God would be kind and that I wouldn't wake up in the morning. Wakening up was the worse thing, knowing that I was still on earth. I hated God in those days. He was just an evil sadistic bully. I had a massive hatred for God and the police and all authority. I jumbled them all together as "them". I just hated "them". It was "they" who had caused all my troubles and if a policeman or a social worker or a Minister or God himself had come anywhere near me, they would be right to fear for their lives. There, by the canal side, I cried a lot and thought about the mess everything was in. My mind went back to chasing rabbits' tails in Bettyhill. Those were happier days but when a father dies you can't bring him back. As I learned early on in my life what's done is done and you can never go back.

By the fifth day, beside the canal bank, I was starting to go mad. I was cold and filthy and so lonely. It hurt. It was not possible to feel more alone than I felt right then.

It took all of those five days for me, like Jonah in the Bible, to admit my need of help. Pride is a terrible thing and causes wars and suicide and mountains of self-pity. I needed to get rid of some pride right then and there. Then, maybe, my life could be saved.

I started walking the long journey back to Beechwood. It was not really very far but for me it was like climbing Everest both because of the physical pain my body was in and because of the embarrassment I felt at admitting to the folk at Beechwood I had failed. I thought that they probably would reject me, even be angry with me and I would have understood. Because I kept stopping in doubt and fear of how I would be received, it took me many hours to walk the two miles to Beechwood.

When eventually I arrived one of the staff came out and studied my face. I thought he would tell me to leave and I think he wanted to but first he fetched Iain the manager. Iain came outside to me and said quietly, "I heard what happened" and he hugged me. For a long long time he hugged me.

I started crying and all that anger inside me subsided and he started crying too.

Nowadays in these times when the rulebook rules everything, there would be very little chance of them accepting me back, but, on that particular day, Iain was brave enough to break a rule or two when it needed to be broken. This saved my life. He told me I had to go back into the drying-out process again. After that, I went back to the sixteen week programme. I was in Beechwood for a total of 22 weeks but I never drank again. That was seventeen years ago.

Afterword

Help Support Geoff's outreach work

There were a few people who helped Geoff. There were John and Janet Marshall who treated him like an adopted son and his cousins Marion and Rab Anthony were good to him. They listened to him and visited him every day in Beechwood. There were others too. These sort of people are special and really helped him remain sober in those first difficult months.

All the work he has done in the past few years has been to help the homeless and those suffering from addiction. He was for a time in charge of the homeless night shelter in Inverness but this was closed down by one of the Titans. Apparently kindness is not the duty of the council. Theirs was the business of rules, regulations and officiousness. Geoff was not a happy pen pusher. What would you expect? He'd only just taught himself to read.

The way he taught himself to read was like this. He had to read three pages of a book for a meeting. It took him four months to read the pages but after four months he read them publicly at a meeting. Suddenly the fear of reading was gone and Geoff can now read quite well.

A Big Issue salesman called Kevin, who is now part of our project, once gave Geoff a scruffy piece of paper with a telephone number on it. This turned out to be my number

Geoff and I met and tramped round the area for nearly six months before we had the courage to take out a lease on 60 Grant St and start a charity shop, which would fund a befriending scheme to help addicts in Merkinch.

Many people joined us and, with the help of our newly found Trustees, we managed to get a Big Lottery Grant for the past five years. This money is now running out but we are trying as hard as we can to fund the project with our own efforts and to be able to fund Geoff's outreach work.

Geoff is remarried now and get on well with my grown up children who are both working and doing well.

One of the people helping to put this book together is his younger brother Paul who has been sober now for more than four years. His other brother died in 1999 after an alcoholic fit.

For the past five years Geoff has been in charge of the outreach work to alcoholics and has had some considerable success in helping folk quit alcohol. One of the reasons for producing this book is that Geoff's crucial funding has now run out. We called ourselves For The Right Reasons because, above all, we wanted our work to be motivated by kindness and understanding towards addicts instead of the world's condemnation.

We hope that this little book will help people understand the terrible illness of alcohol addiction and the huge importance of Geoff's work in the community. Every penny of profit raised by this book and every penny donated as a result of reading this book will be put towards Geoff's outreach work to recovering addicts in Inverness.

Rev Richard Burkitt
Director
For The Right Reasons
www.fortherightreasons.net